the

CHINESE
BRIDE'S GUIDE
TO MARRYING IN AUSTRALIA

ABOUT THE SERIES

Something Different Wedding Guides are comprehensive guides, created for the couple who value tradition but do not want to being either constrained or intimidated by it. Each guide addresses a contemporary issue in wedding planning.

DISCLAIMER

Although Jennifer Cram has taken every care in preparing and writing this book, she accepts no liability for any errors, omissions, misuse, or misunderstanding on the part of any person who uses it. Reliance on the material in this book shall be at your sole risk. The author specifically disclaims any implied warranty of fitness for any particular purpose and accepts no responsibility for any damage, injury, or loss occasioned to any person as a result of relying on any material included, omitted, or implied.

the

CHINESE
BRIDE'S GUIDE

TO MARRYING IN AUSTRALIA

JENNIFER CRAM

Authorized Marriage celebrant

Something Different Wedding Guides

ISBN-10: 1518724604
ISBN-13: 978-1518724602

Something Old
Something New
Something Borrowed
Something Blue
Something Different

CONTENTS

1 INTRODUCTION

Australians are very accepting of intercultural marriages and of incorporating traditions from other cultures in weddings. In addition, getting married in Australia is in many ways very simple and easy.

However, unlike in China and some other Asian countries where it is the couple that register the marriage by going to the government office to sign the marriage papers, in Australia it is the celebrant who must register the marriage.

Therefore, you must have a formal ceremony, led by a celebrant authorized by the Australian Government to solemnise the marriage, and you must sign marriage papers as part of the ceremony.

For brides newly arrived in Australia, for Chinese brides marrying Australian grooms, or for Chinese couples marrying in Australia and wishing to have a Western style wedding, what is legally required, and what is local custom can sometimes be a little confusing.

I hope you will find this book a useful aid to marrying in Australia, and that you have a fabulous day.

2 THE MOST IMPORTANT THING TO KNOW ABOUT GETTING MARRIED IN AUSTRALIA

You must comply with all the Legal Requirements of the Marriage Act.

- **You must give notice of your intention to marry.**
  You must complete a *Notice of Intended Marriage*, sign it in front of a qualified witness (your celebrant is a qualified witness), and give it to your celebrant at least a month ahead of the big day. **NB the *Notice* is kept by the celebrant until after the wedding, then it is sent in to Births, Deaths, and Marriages (a government entity) with the rest of the papers to register your marriage.**

- **Both of you must show your celebrant all the required proofs of identity and date and place of birth and, if relevant, proof of how your previous marriage ended.** All of these documents must be the **original** documents as issued by the relevant government authority. If any of these documents are not in English you will be required to provide official translations in English.

- **You both must sign legal declarations that you are free to marry.**

This must happen close to but before the ceremony takes place.

- **You must give real consent**
  This means that if at any time in the lead up to the ceremony or during the ceremony itself, you say or do anything (even as a joke) that could cast doubt on whether you are getting married of your own free will, the celebrant cannot legally continue with the wedding.

- **You must be able to understand the ceremony**
  If you do not understand English sufficiently to understand the ceremony and the legal requirements for marrying that you have to meet before your marriage can take place, you will be required to have an interpreter who can translate for you and for the celebrant.

During the ceremony

- **You must be sober**
  While one or two alcoholic drinks before the ceremony won't cause any problems, if your celebrant considers that you are sufficiently impaired by alcohol, medication, or illegal substances that questions could be raised as to your capacity to know what you are doing, the celebrant is required by law not to proceed with the wedding.

- **You must have two adult witnesses present**
  As long as they are at least 18, legally sane, mentally competent and neither drunk nor under the influence of drugs or medications, and they are capable of seeing, hearing, and understanding the legal nature of the ceremony, there are no requirements as to who they are:
  - They can be blood relatives
  - They can be friends
  - If you are eloping your witnesses can be hotel, restaurant, or wedding venue staff, or strangers off the street.

- They do not have to be your best man and chief bridesmaid. While that is traditional for bigger weddings, more and more couples are honoring their mothers, grandparents, other relatives or friends by requesting them to act as their witnesses

- **Your celebrant has to make the statement required by Section 46 of the Marriage Act:**
  I am duly authorized by law to solemnise marriages according to law. Before you are joined together in marriage in my presence and in the presence of these witnesses, I am to remind you of the solemn and binding nature of the relationship into which you are now about to enter. Marriage, according to law in Australia, is the union of a man and a woman to the exclusion of all others, voluntarily entered into for life.

- **You have to say, out loud and individually, the statement that creates your marriage.**
  Yes, that's right, before you've even put pen to paper you are legally married.

- **Your full names must be said at least once in the ceremony.**

- **On the certificates and during the ceremony, names are in Western order (Family Name last).**
  If you are known by an English name that can be said as well as your legal Chinese first name, but not instead of it, unless the English name is also on your birth certificate (as sometimes happens if you were born in Hong Kong, for example).

At the end of the ceremony

- **You and your witnesses must sign the marriage papers (the certificates and the Register)**
  These papers document that the marriage has taken place.
- **Bride and groom sign first**
  You should use your normal signatures (i.e. those you used on the *Notice of Intended Marriage*) and on your *Declarations*.

If you normally sign using Chinese characters, you may sign your marriage papers that way.

The bride does **not** sign in her married name. **She uses her maiden name (her name at birth)** or the name she has been previously known by if she was married before and did not revert to her maiden name.

- **The witnesses sign after the bride and groom**

- **Your Celebrant signs last.**

3 EIGHT OTHER IMPORTANT THINGS TO KNOW ABOUT GETTING MARRIED IN AUSTRALIA

1. **You can have your ceremony where you wish**
   Apart from obvious Health and Safety considerations, there are **no** restrictions on where you hold the ceremony:

   - It can be in a public place, such as a park, a restaurant, or a chapel, or in a private place, such as your own home or a hotel suite with the doors closed.
   - The place does not have to be licensed to host weddings, nor does it have to have a fixed roof (though shade is a very good idea as is having a good alternative Plan B in case of extreme heat or bad weather).
   - It can be in the air (as long as it is in Australian air space) or at sea (as long as it is within Australian waters).

2. **You can have your ceremony when you wish**
   You will be able to be married on the most auspicious day and at the most auspicious time because there are **no**

restrictions on what time of the day or day of the year you get married,

- You can be married any time of day or night
- You can be married on any day of the week
- You can be married on a public holiday, including religious holidays and days of national significance, so if Good Friday, Christmas Day, Australia Day or Anzac Day falls on the most auspicious day for your wedding, the law allows you to marry, and wedding service providers will be available.

3. **You may include religious content if you wish**
Unlike the UK, where mention of anything religious is forbidden in a civil wedding, or the US, where religious content is common in civil weddings, in Australia you can have religious content if you wish, but it is a personal choice. The celebrant cannot force you to include or exclude religious content. In addition, the celebrant is not allowed to include religious content without your express request.

4. **You do not have to observe or include outdated customs that relegate the bride to second-class status**

- The bride does **not** have to be "given away" (we can ask both sets of parents for their support instead - but of course that doesn't mean you can't walk down the aisle on your father's arm.
- The bride is **not** required to promise to obey

5. **You do not have to stand with your backs to your guests**
There is no altar, so no-one has to face it with their backs to the guests. In Australia, the bridal party usually faces the guests for part of the ceremony. The bride and groom face one another to make their vows and exchange rings.

6. **The Pronouncement**

   Having your celebrant declare that you are married is a tradition - but it has **no** legal effect. You probably won't want to skip it, but if you want to take a non-traditional approach to it, that's fine.

7. **You do not have to kiss**

   The kiss is a western wedding tradition **not** a legal requirement. If it is culturally uncomfortable for you to kiss in front of others, there is no problem with skipping the kiss. Some couples choose to hug. Others rely on the celebrant to smoothly move to the signing.

8. **Getting married does not automatically change the bride's surname**

   If you want to change your surname to that of your new spouse (yes, the groom can change his name to the bride's if he wishes). It is easy to do so - you just start calling yourself by your preferred surname and then follow up by changing your name on all of your ID documentation, however

   - Your name is **not** changed automatically
   - You are not required to change your surname to that of your husband
   - If you decide to change your name, you can just call yourself by your new name (Mrs....) but you will then need to change your name on all your official documents – your driver license, your passport, and so on.
   - You need to have the official Marriage Certificate from Births, Deaths and Marriage in the state in which you married to prove that you are married and can therefore do a name change by marriage.

4 FEDERAL AND STATE RESPONSIBILITIES

Australia is unusual in that both the Commonwealth Government, and the governments of the individual Australian states and territories have a role in marriage.

The Marriage Act is a federal law that covers all states and territories, so the requirements are the same regardless of where in Australia you marry.

However, because Australia was established as a number of individual colonies, registration of births, deaths, and marriages is the responsibility of the individual states and territories.

You can choose to be married in one of three different ways.

1. Civil celebrants are appointed by the Commonwealth Government, and can marry you anywhere in Australia.

2. Marriage officers are state or territory government employees and can marry you in the Registry Office or a courthouse in each state or territory, with the exception of the Australian Capital Territory where the Registry Office no longer performs marriages.

3. Clergy and religious leaders who are licensed to perform marriages (not all are) can marry you in their church or temple or other designated religious site. Some religions also allow their clergy to marry couples at other venues or in a park or garden.

5 THE AUSTRALIAN WEDDING CEREMONY

While many Australian couples do have a fairly traditional wedding ceremony, it is socially acceptable to have a less formal ceremony.

This also includes your bridal party. You may include as many or as few people as you wish, you may mix genders on both bride's and groom's side, and you may include or omit any of the roles. So you don't want a small boy carrying the rings down the aisle? That's fine. Want only one bridesmaid, but two best men? That's fine too. It is up to you.

Elements of the Traditional Wedding Ceremony as performed by a Civil Celebrant

The traditional Western wedding ceremony originated as a church wedding. A traditional wedding ceremony, as performed by a civil celebrant in Australia, contains all the elements of the traditional Christian wedding, with the exception of prayers, blessings, bible readings, and hymns. Readings from non-religious books or poetry may be included in the civil celebrant wedding, but are not a requirement.

Processional (the formal walk in)

Welcome and Introduction

Affirmation of Parents/ Presentation of the Bride
(and in modern practice, also of the Groom)

Celebrant's Statement from the Marriage Act
(Legally required statement by the celebrant in a civil marriage.
It is often referred to as *The Monitum* and is not required in a
religious marriage ceremony conducted by a member of the
clergy)

Reflections on Marriage (by the celebrant)

Affirmation of Intent
(The *I Will*/*I Do* Statements)

Vows

Exchange of Rings

Pronouncement

The Kiss

Signing of Marriage Certificate and Register

Presentation of Certificate

Recessional (the formal walk out)

The Bridal Party

In a traditional wedding, the bride and groom are supported
by a bridal party. The groom is supported by male attendants
(the groomsmen) and the bride by adult females (the
bridesmaids) and possibly by female children (flower girls),
and/or male children (Page Boys and/or a Ring Bearer).

Each member of the bridal party has a specific role and
specific responsibilities, and these are reflected in the order in
which they walk down the aisle and the order in which they
stand during the ceremony. Usually the groom and his
attendants stand at the front waiting for the bride and her

attendants. The bride's attendants walk down the aisle before the bride. She walks in last with her escort. However, it is becoming more common for the groomsmen to escort the bridesmaids down the aisle, and it is not uncommon for the bride and groom to walk in together.

In the modern Australian version of the traditional wedding some, all, or none of the following roles are represented in the bridal party:

Best Man

The Best Man is not merely the groom's friend, comrade, and witness; he also takes care of many of the practical details related to the wedding. He may keep custody of the bride's ring or of both rings until they are called for in the ceremony. The best man also trouble-shoots when there are last minute hitches with transportation or other arrangements.

Groomsman

Like the role of bridesmaid, that of groomsman is purely decorative during the ceremony, though they can be called upon to assist the best man where remedial action needs to be taken to fix a problem with arrangements. There is usually the same number of groomsmen as bridesmaids, however, this is not a hard and fast rule and, at many weddings, there are fewer groomsmen than bridesmaids.

The Bride's Escort

Traditionally the bride is escorted by her father, who walks down the aisle with her, or her father and mother. However she can be escorted by anyone she chooses, or she can choose to walk in alone.

Chief Bridesmaid

The chief bridesmaid may be call the Maid of Honor (if unmarried) or the Matron of Honor (if married). Traditionally she is the bride's sister or best friend. She acts as the bride's witness. During the ceremony, she holds the bride's bouquet, checks and helps with the bride's veil, makes sure her train is fluffed and attractively arranged, and generally supports the bride. She may also keep custody of the groom's ring until it is called for before the vows.

Bridesmaid(s)

The role of bridesmaid during the ceremony is purely decorative, although where the Chief Bridesmaid needs to have her hands free to arrange the bride's train, she can hand off her bouquet and the bride's bouquet to the next bridesmaid in line. Bridesmaids may also assist with children in the bridal party, if necessary holding the children by the hand as they walk down the aisle.

Junior Bridesmaid

A junior bridesmaid is a girl who is too young to be an adult bridesmaid but too old to be a flower girl. She is usually dressed in a similar fashion to the bridesmaids. Her role is purely decorative, though, like the bridesmaids, she can assist with children in the bridal party.

Flower Girl

Historically children are included in the bridal party to ensure fertility and good fortune. In modern times their role is to add a sentimental connection with childhood. Invariably they also add energy, playfulness, and moments of light-hearted and unplanned humour. If the venue allows it, the flower girl scatters rose petals in the path of the bride.

Page Boy/Train Bearer

Page boys walk behind the bride and carry her train. Including page boys in the processional is a good idea where the bride's train is very long, or the bridal party needs to walk up steps or on garden paths, as the Page Boys hold the train off the ground to enable the bride to walk without the train snagging or pulling her back. Because carrying a train requires some strength, coordination and concentration, page boys should be about 7 to 12 years old.

Ring Bearer

While there is no reason that the ring bearer cannot be a little girl or an adult person of either gender, the ring bearer is usually a small boy, 3 – 5 years of age, though, as with flower girls, this may be too young to be sure of a polished performance. The ring bearer carries the rings on a pillow or in some other form of decorative container.

The Processional

The processional is the formal start to a traditional wedding ceremony. The bride, escorted by her father or other person, and accompanied by bridesmaids and perhaps one or more flower girls, Ring Bearers and Page Boys, enters the church, chapel, or ceremony space and walks down the aisle, through the guests, to take her place next to the groom.

In Australia, the bridesmaids usually walk down the aisle before the bride. The chief bridesmaid is the last of the bridesmaids to walk down the aisle. If there is a flower girl and/or ring bearer they walk down the aisle after the chief bridesmaid and just before the bride.

Walking Down the Aisle

As a celebrant I see what the groom sees as you walk down the aisle. You want to make this the ultimate Wow! moment for him, so read on for everything you need to know about walking down the aisle with style, grace and confidence.

Which side?

If your father or someone else is going to walk you down the aisle put your palm on the inside of his forearm and fold your fingers over the top/front to show off your fingernails. Which arm is a personal choice. In traditional Christian weddings a bride walks on her father's left side (this is to leave his sword arm free to draw his sword and defend her if necessary – something I've never had to do in hundreds and hundreds of wedding). However, it does leave his right hand free to shake the groom's hand.

How to walk?

You've been walking normally all your life. Yet there is still a belief out there in wedding land that there is a special (silly) walk for the aisle. Forget it. Stroll, even saunter, but do not do the hesitation step (aka stagger step) where you take a step and then bring your feet together before you take another step. It looks silly, is very difficult to do in high heels, and is almost guaranteed to make you wobble and even fall over.

Where a couple is having a small wedding, it is very common for the bride not to make a formal entrance. Instead the bride, groom, and their witnesses take their places at the front of the ceremony space with the celebrant when ready to start the ceremony.

Affirmation of Parents/ Presentation of Bride

In the very traditional wedding the bride was 'given away' to the groom by her father or other male relative. In the 21st century, this is regarded to be inappropriate. The modern version of the tradition is for the celebrant to ask the parents of both the bride and the groom for their support and blessing on the marriage.

Affirmation of Intent

Traditionally, both the bride and groom are asked if they will accept one another as husband and wife. These questions are not the legal vows.

Vows

To be legally married in Australia, each of you must make a statement, using the required legal words, that you ask everyone present to witness that you take one another to be your husband or wife.

Exchange of Rings

In Australia, wedding rings are worn on the ring finger (the one next to your little finger /pinkie) of the left hand of both bride and groom. It is usual to exchange wedding rings after your vows.

To ensure that the ring exchange goes smoothly there are two things you need to do.

First, you need to decide what to do with your engagement ring. Traditionally, the wedding ring is worn closest to your palm with your engagement ring closer to your fingertip, so generally a bride will move her engagement ring to her right hand before the ceremony and put it back on her left hand afterwards. However, if it your engagement ring does not fit on your right ring finger (which is not uncommon) you can give it to someone else to look after. Some options are

- give it to the best man who can return it at the signing table (just make sure it is in a little pouch or some other container to ensure it won't get lost or dropped), or
- ask your mother, mother-in-law, or other female you wish to honor to mind it during the ceremony and then give it back to you after the ceremony.

Secondly, you need to make sure your hand is bare ready to receive the ring. In China it is very common for a bride to wear gloves with her wedding dress. Australian brides almost never wear gloves.

However, if you choose to wear gloves you will need to either take your glove off before the vows and ring exchange (give it to your chief bridesmaid to hold), or unpick the stitches in the ring finger of your left glove, so that it can be pushed out of the way to bare your finger.

The Pronouncement

It is traditional that the celebrant announces that you are now husband and wife. This is not a legal requirement and the statement does not create your marriage. By the time it is made, you are already legally married.

The Kiss

The kiss after you have been pronounced husband and wife is a big deal part of the wedding in Australia but it is not compulsory. You will still be married whether you kiss or not. In multicultural Australia no one will expect you to kiss if you find that culturally uncomfortable.

The Signing

The bride, groom, the two witnesses and the celebrant must all sign the Marriage Register, the Marriage Certificate and the Presentation Certificate to document that you have said your vows and created your marriage. It is usual to have photographs taken of this moment.

The Presentation of the Certificate

At the end of the ceremony you will be presented with a certificate that has the Australian Coat of Arms on it. It is proof you are married, but if you plan to apply for a visa, or need proof of marriage for other purposes, such as changing your name to that of your new husband, you will need to apply for and obtain an official certificate from Births, Deaths and Marriages in the state in which you married. Your celebrant will explain how to do this.

The Recessional

At the end of the formal traditional ceremony the bridal party, lead by the bride and groom, followed by the rest of the bridal party in couples, walks back down the aisle between the guests. Many couples now choose not to have a formal recessional. Instead, the celebrant invites the guests to come forward to congratulate them.

6 CELEBRATING YOUR CHINESE HERITAGE IN YOUR AUSTRALIAN WEDDING

Chinese customs have been part of the Australian multicultural experience since the 19th century. The first recorded Chinese born settler was a man named Ahuto, a carpenter who came to Australia as a free man in 1803. The first record we have of a Chinese-Australian intercultural wedding is that of Mak Sai Ying (also known as John Pong Shying), another Chinese-born settler, who married Sarah Jane Thompson on 3 February 1823 in St John's Church of England, Parramatta.

Chinese people are considered to be the oldest continuous immigrants to Australia outside of those from Great Britain. As a result Australians are comfortable with Chinese food and with Chinese concepts around lucky colors, lucky symbols, and lucky items. In addition, Australian weddings are full of customs and traditions that are all about good luck for the couple. So adding Chinese customs to your Australian wedding will not only be accepted by Australian guests and family members, they will be valued and enjoyed.

Australian brides happily adapt traditions to suit their personalities and their vision for their wedding. Rather than being unusual the personal touch and the different approach is the norm. It is expected that couples will personalize their wedding, and there is no better way to do that than to celebrate your heritage.

In an intercultural wedding both heritages are celebrated, and there are many options to celebrate your Chinese heritage within an Australian wedding.

Honoring the Elders
The Western tradition of giving away the bride has largely been replaced by a request by the celebrant to the parents for their support for the marriage. This is a point in the ceremony where the bride and groom can honor their parents in accordance with Chinese tradition.

Using Both Languages
While, generally speaking, wedding ceremonies in Australia are conducted in English, it is perfectly legal to use other languages. Where English is not the first language of the bride, the groom, or both bride and groom, I always suggest that they fulfill the legal requirements by making their vows in English, and then repeat their promises in their first language.

I consider this to be particularly important when family members or friends who do not understand English are present.

Where the bride or groom has limited English, an interpreter will be required.

You can also request your celebrant to include a moment in the ceremony when you can just speak from the heart to one another, using whichever language you wish.

Using Red
Although the traditional wedding dress color for an Australian bride is white, nowadays white can mean anything from white (which comes in a very large number of tones), to

ivory, to cream, to ecru, to oyster, to coffee. But Australian brides are free to choose to wear a formal wedding gown in any color. Wearing red is not uncommon.

Alternatively, adding color in the form of a sash, train insert, embroidery is also common. And an emerging trend is for colorful additions to be hidden, until the bride lifts her skirt to reveal her shoes. I've had brides celebrate their Irish heritage by wearing green shoes, add a touch of tartan to celebrate their Scottish heritage by wearing shoes covered in their or their groom's clan tartan, incorporate *Something Blue* by wearing blue shoes, or wear red shoes either as an expression of exuberance or to acknowledge their Chinese heritage. And on a number of occasions a bride has lifted the hem of her skirt to reveal beautifully embroidered Moroccan or Chinese wedding slippers.

Including Visual Symbols

The Double-Happiness character is widely recognized in Australia, and the symbolism of oranges is likewise understood thanks to participation of Australians in Chinese New Year celebrations. So feel free to use either or both in your ceremony décor or reception decoration. I recently officiated at a garden wedding where potted dwarf orange trees in red pots marked the aisle.

When Queen Victoria wore a wreath of orange blossoms at her wedding in 1840, she set the classic floral theme for English brides throughout the 19th and into the early 20th century. As Australian brides generally followed English traditions, virtually every Australian bride also wore orange blossoms.

While most probably did not realize that incorporating orange blossoms in the bride's costume originated in China, understanding of the symbolism of the orange tree as one of the rare plants that bears blossoms and fruit at the same time has survived, signifying prosperity, good luck, fertility, and happiness.

7 WEDDING MUSIC

Music adds a great deal to the wedding. Many couples use recorded music, others use live musicians playing. Music is not played during the actual ceremony as that interferes with people being able to hear the words being spoken.

Music is played

- before the ceremony starts, while the guests are gathering. This music tends to be soft and romantic.
- for the Processional (formal entrance of the bride and her bridesmaids). This music is more upbeat, and at a pace that is easy to walk in to.
- during the Signing of the Register and Certificates. Again this music is relatively soft, but can be either instrumental or songs. You need at least three pieces of music because there are a number of people signing, and your photographer usually spends some time taking photographs of the signing and some posed photos of your hands on the certificate.
- for the Recessional (the formal exit of the bride, groom and Bridal Party), choose really upbeat, happy music that is at a faster pace than the Processional music.

8 WHAT SHOULD EVERYONE WEAR?

For a traditional wedding the bride, the groom, the bridal party and the guests all dress formally.

The bride will usually wear a long white, ivory, or cream wedding dress with a train and a veil., but this is not a hard and fast rule. Increasingly brides are wearing pastel colors, and even red. The groom will wear a suit or dinner suit. The bridesmaids will wear long colored dresses without a train. The groomsmen will dress in a similar fashion to the groom, but with perhaps a different colored tie or vest (waistcoat).

If you are marrying outdoors in a park or garden, everyone dresses less formally. For practical reasons, it is usual that the bride's gown does not have a long train, and may have no train.

But it is also acceptable in Australia to dress as casually as you like. You may wish to wear a street-length dress rather than a full-length one. And the groom may choose to wear dress trousers and a nice shirt in order to be more comfortable.

It is your choice. No-one will judge you!

One Dress or Two ... or Three ...

Because Australian brides buy their dresses rather than hire them, it is usual to have only one dress and to wear that dress for both the ceremony and the reception. Where the ceremony dress is very elaborate, a small proportion of Australian brides will have a second, much simpler dress to wear for the latter part of the reception in order to be able to party on the dance floor.

If you wish to wear a white wedding dress for the ceremony and then change to a red dress, a cheongsam, or something else, that would not be regarded to be unusual. Changing your dress more than once, however, would be.

Colors

While some older Australians still have reservations about women wearing black to a wedding, any and all colors are acceptable. It is now not uncommon for bridesmaids or guests to wear black. Even brides can, and on occasion, do choose to wear a black wedding dress or a wedding dress featuring back embroidery or other trim.

The men in the bridal party most commonly wear black suits, with dark navy a close second However, fashion forward grooms are also choosing other colors for themselves and their attendants. So we see light colored suits (sensible in the hotter months), white suits, and brightly colored suits. I've officiated at weddings where the groom wore a hot pink suit, where both bride and groom wore white, where both bride and groom wore black, where the bride wore red and the groom black with a white shirt and a red tie, and numerous weddings where the groom wore a brightly colored or patterned shirt in every color of the rainbow.

It is usual for the men in the bridal party to echo the color of the bridesmaids' dresses in the color of their ties.

Alternatives to Matching Dresses for the Bridesmaids

The most common choice is for all of the bridesmaids to wear identical dresses, but things are changing. Brides are choosing a color and allowing the bridesmaids to each choose a style that will suit their particular body type. As long as hemlines are the same (long, short, or calf-length), this works beautifully – and makes for happy bridesmaids.

Another emerging trend is different shades of the same color.

Alternatives to the Formal Suit for the Men

Australians tend to be relatively casual in dress. So a groom marrying wearing a formal suit but with no tie is quite common. Marrying wearing a sports coat and pants, or pants, shirt, tie, and braces (suspenders), likewise is an emerging trend (pin the boutonniere to the braces, not the shirt) as is pants, shirt, tie, and vest (waistcoat). The groom may wear a suit with the groomsmen wearing matching pants, shirts, ties, and either vests or braces.

For a less formal wedding dress jeans or chinos and a collared long-sleeve shirt is a choice that some grooms are making.

Very Informal Weddings

There is nothing in the Marriage Act that dictates the look and feel for your wedding. So choosing to have a very casual and informal wedding is both legally and socially acceptable in Australia.

In short, what you wear is a personal choice, to a certain extent driven by the type of wedding you choose to have. A formal wedding requires formal clothing. A less formal wedding opens the way to wearing anything you wish.

9 WEDDING TRADITIONS

Most of the wedding traditions observed in Australian weddings are common to most English-speaking countries in the western world. Many of the older generation continue to suggest that including these traditions is the only way to have a 'proper' wedding.

The origins of most of these traditions are no longer known or understood, and really, whether you choose to include them, ignore them, or decide to include a Chinese tradition instead, is entirely your choice. In our multicultural society, we are used to acknowledging, including, and celebrating a mix of traditions as chosen by couples for their wedding.

Western Wedding Traditions

The following wedding traditions are common in Australia but are not observed in all weddings:

Bride wearing a formal white gown

This is a relatively new tradition – copied from Queen Victoria! Bridal gowns now come in all colors, including red, white, blue, ivory, the color of a latte coffee, and even black. They can be formal, or short, simple, vintage or cutting edge fashion. Some brides even wear costumes to go with a theme wedding.

The bride having *Something Old, Something New, Something Borrowed, Something Blue*, on her on the day.

Something Old represents the bride's link with her family and with the past. It is often a family heirloom that has been passed down through the generations, and is generally a piece of jewelry.

Something New represents the new life ahead as a married woman. This is generally the bride's dress, but if the bride has chosen to wear a vintage or heirloom gown, it can be her hairpiece or other item.

Something Borrowed is usually an item of jewelry borrowed from a happily married woman, and is thought to ensure her future happiness.

Something Blue. The color blue has for many centuries represented faithfulness and loyalty. Traditionally a tiny blue ribbon bow was sewn inside the bride's dress, but your something blue can be anything you wish – from blue shoes to blue jewelry, or even a blue dress.

Best Man and Chief Bridesmaid as Witnesses

While traditionally a good friend of the bride acts as the chief bridesmaid and as her legal witness, and a good friend of the groom acts as the best man and as his legal witness, more and more couples are choosing other people, not part of the bridal party, to be their legal witnesses and sign the marriage register and certificate. Any adult you wish to honor can act as your witness, as long as they are able to understand the ceremony

Giving Away of the Bride

The old tradition where the celebrant asks *Who gives this woman to be married to this man?* Modern couples recognize that the bride is not the possession of her father and that she has chosen freely to marry the groom so omit this.

Throwing of Rice or Confetti

This old tradition, where the guests threw uncooked rice or paper confetti over the bride and groom as they exited the church or ceremony space, has all but disappeared. Most venues, including parks, do not allow the throwing of rice or confetti. Some places allow the throwing of rose petals, and others the blowing of bubbles. But many also band one or both of these. Most venues that ban the throwing of rice, confetti, or roses, and/or the blowing of bubbles will fine the couple a large amount of money if any guests ignore the ban.

The Groom not seeing the Bride before the Wedding

Another old tradition is that the groom should not see the bride on the day of the wedding before she walks down the aisle. So many couples spend the night staying in different places. This tradition grew up in the days of arranged weddings to guard against the groom deciding not to go ahead with the wedding because he didn't think the bride was pretty enough!

More and more couples are having photographs taken together before the wedding. And staging a *first look* is a growing trend.

The Bouquet Toss/Garter Toss

The tradition of the bride tossing her bouquet to the single women, with the one who catches it said to be the next female to marry, is an old tradition that does not really fit with modern life. The groom removing the bride's garter from her leg, either by reaching under her dress with his hands or by putting his head under her skirt and removing the garter with his teeth, is regarded by many Australians to be embarrassing and degrading to the bride. The old tradition was that the garter is thrown to the unmarried men, with the one who catches it said to be the next male to marry. Many brides are now tossing their bouquet towards all the unmarried guests, both male and female, and are skipping the garter throw. A growing number of brides are also skipping the bouquet throw, choosing instead to present their bouquet to their mother, grandmother, or other honored woman as an expression of love and respect.

Australian Wedding Traditions

There are very few wedding traditions that are unique to Australia.

Acknowledging the Traditional Owners

The protocol of respectfully acknowledging the traditional owners of the land on which an event is being held is observed at public and government-sponsored gatherings. This tradition has its roots in the 60,000 year history of indigenous culture on the Australian continent. It is becoming quite common to acknowledge the traditional owners at the start of a wedding. The celebrant will do this at your request.

Stone Ceremony

The stone ceremony is a tradition that originated in the early days of European settlement of Australia, possibly with convicts sent from England and Ireland as punishment for their crimes. Because these couples could not afford wedding rings, they would each throw a stone into a river, lake, dam, or the ocean to seal their vows and as a symbol of their commitment to stay together forever as life ebbed and flowed around them. The custom reflects the Celtic tradition of throwing objects into water as an offering to spirits.

10 WEDDING PHOTOGRAPHY

Wedding photography in Australia happens on the day of the wedding, not before.

Wedding photographers offer a range of packages so you may choose to have a photographer present from early morning in order to take photographs of both bride and groom getting ready, or you may choose to have the professional photographer arrive after your hair and makeup is complete.

Most brides in Australia still follow the tradition of the groom not seeing them in the wedding dress before the ceremony. However, a significant proportion of couples are scheduling the taking of formal posed photographs of the bridal party before the ceremony in order to free up time to spend with guests.

To be able to do this while still preserving the magic moment when the groom sees the bride in her dress for the first time, photographers are suggesting a "first look" photo session.

How this works is that the groom waits for the bride in some private location such as the garden of the venue where the ceremony is being held. On cue the bride walks up behind him whereupon he turns for the first look, all captured in a series of photographs by the photographer. The formal photographs follow, and then the groom makes his way to the ceremony venue, allowing the bride and her attendants to follow when it is time for the ceremony to start and the bride to make her entrance.

11 MONEY GIFTS

While lucky red packets are not a feature of Australian weddings, wishing wells are rapidly becoming almost the norm.

Wishing wells are a way of signaling to the guests that the couple would prefer money gifts over toasters, towels, or other household goods.

How they work is that the couple includes mention of the wishing well and a request for money as a gift with the invitation sent to guests. At the reception a wishing well is placed in a prominent place and guests can put greeting cards containing a check or cash in the wishing well.

12 THANK YOU NOTES AND TESTIMONIALS

In Australia it is considered good manners to write a personal thank-you to every person who gave you a wedding gift or sent a card, and to do it as quickly after the wedding as possible.

Many couples have special cards made featuring a photograph from the wedding.

It is also considered good manners to thank the various suppliers of the services that made your wedding. That your wedding went smoothly is down to your wedding suppliers. Much of what they do goes unnoticed because it is their job to fix problems before they become problems.

And you can also show your appreciation by taking the time to complete any feedback forms your vendors might have given you, and to write a testimonial that can be posted on their website or used in advertising.

No doubt you used the comments made by previous couples to help you choose your various wedding service suppliers. So you should repay the favor.

13 YOUR MARRIAGE CERTIFICATE

On the day of your marriage you will be issued with a Presentation Certificate. It is a legal document that includes the Australian coat of arms, so it is proof that you are married, but it is not proof that your marriage has been registered.

An official marriage certificate, which is proof that your marriage has been registered, can be obtained from Births, Deaths, and Marriages in the State or Territory in which you married. It is important to note that your official marriage certificate is not issued automatically.

Your celebrant will submit the marriage papers to Births, Deaths, and Marriages in the state in which you were married for registration of your marriage.

After your marriage has been registered (which may take several weeks) you will need to make formal application for a copy of this certificate. The fee for the certificate is set by each state, and differs from state to state.

14 CHANGING YOUR NAME

In Australia both the bride and the groom are able to change their name by marriage. However, this is not a requirement and it does not happen automatically.

Traditionally the bride has taken the groom's surname (last name) on marriage, but a groom may take the bride's surname, and quite a few do. Alternatively, the bride can add the groom's name to hers in a hyphenated name, or the couple can both adopt a hyphenated name consisting of both names, or they can both keep the names they had before marriage.

It is a personal choice.

If you choose to change your name by marriage, all you need to do is start calling yourself by that surname (last name), and when you receive your official marriage certificate you can then begin changing your name on your various official documents.

If you also wish to change you given name(s) for example, taking a Western name instead of, or as well as, your Chinese name, you will need to apply to Births, Deaths, and Marriages in the state in which you are living for a legal change of name.

15 SECOND CEREMONY

Australian law allows a couple to have only one legal marriage ceremony.

However, this does not stop couples from having a non-legal religious or cultural ceremony.

So if you wish to travel back to China or another country to celebrate with family and friends and have a cultural ceremony or a religious ceremony, this is legally allowable as long as no legal paperwork is done, and the marriage is not registered again.

You may also have a non-legal religious or cultural ceremony in Australia or elsewhere.

ABOUT THE AUTHOR

Jennifer Cram is an award-winning professional marriage celebrant (wedding officiant) appointed by the Attorney General to officiate marriages in all states and territories of Australia. She is currently based in Brisbane, Queensland, where each year she creates and officiates at in excess of one hundred ceremonies, including many ceremonies where the bride is Chinese.

Her couples have consistently voted her one of the top celebrants in the country since 2009 and in 2013 she was named Queensland's top celebrant in the Australian Bridal Industry Academy Awards.

www.jennifercram.com.au

www.ingramcontent.com/pod-product-compliance
Lightning Source LLC
Chambersburg PA
CBHW071143280525
45787CB00003B/1389